FROM 25 REJECTIONS TO A MILLION READERS

ESSENTIAL TIPS FOR BUDDING AUTHORS

BRONNIE WARE

ISBN: 978-0-6459351-0-3

Published by Platypus Creek Publishing, Australia.

CONTENTS

INTRODUCTION

DON'T WAIT FOR PERFECTION TO GET YOUR WORK OUT THERE

I'm not the best author on the planet. You don't need to be either. That doesn't mean I'm here to encourage you to put unfinished work out there, or a book that only satisfies you, without considering what enjoyment or benefit it will bring to your audience. I'm definitely here to support your most polished work entering the public sphere, sooner rather than later. But I'm also here to make the path to that easier and more enjoyable.

Your voice is unique. If you have the courage to share that and refine your individual expression through writing, then your work will have the capacity to touch the hearts of an appreciative audience.

My three published books have supported my life financially for over a decade, which is a dream come true. So I'm here to share the many things I've learnt about publishing, to help the book waiting inside of you or sitting in a folder on your computer to venture out into the world.

I cannot count how many people have told me over the years that they want to write a book, yet don't. They're waiting to be perfect, or for it to be the "right" time in their life. These are the people who are going to experience the pain of regret later ... and I know a lot about regrets.

Eight years of my life were spent by the bedsides of dying people, as their caregiver. Although there were physical duties included in the role, like showering people who were too weak to look after themselves, wiping the backsides of those too ill to stay awake, or feeding puréed food to someone who could no longer lift a spoon in their last days, I discovered that my main role was to listen. It soon became obvious that regrets were something that people who were dying often reflected on.

When life called me to write about those years, it seemed I was writing about a topic the world was ready for. It started with a blog listing the top five regrets of the dying. When I'd been listening to regrets from the deathbeds and ensuring I didn't end up in the same position myself, I had no idea others needed to hear them too. It was by honouring the requests of some of my dying patients to share their mistakes, so others could learn from them, that their words became public through me. Prior to my time working in palliative care, I also had a long history of deep dissatisfaction with work. These factors were the motivation for me to write.

That blog about the regrets of the dying went ridiculously viral, landing my writing in the public sphere. That blog also became the foundation of my first published book.

In these pages, I'll share my publishing journey with you, including mistakes and joys. This book will also answer questions you might not know to ask yet.

It might be easy to think that what happened to me could never happen to you. I didn't think it could happen to me either. I was, and still am, a freestyle author, following very few rules. I have no writing qualifications from university and first drew on my 1984 high school English lessons to help get me through – classes I actually paid little attention to since I was planning on being a mathematics teacher or a policewoman. (Within a few years, I was working in the banking industry and married to a drug dealer instead.)

I've taken a few short writing courses in fiction in recent years, as it's an area I'm curious to explore and challenge myself in. With three non-fiction books published since that viral blog, I've also worked with editors provided by my publisher. So my writing has now improved well beyond my high school skills. Yours will too. When I put my first book out into the world, though, I was writing more from bravery than skill.

If I'd worried about rules too much, that first book would never have reached the readers it did: over a million people in 32 languages. I've also sold the film rights to it, and it is still shared by word of mouth every day around the globe. Not bad for a book that's already over a decade old and was rejected by 25 publishers.

My case may sound unique and impossible, but publishing your work is more about courage and accepting that you'll make mistakes. It's how we learn. If you're willing to have a go, then these pages may save you from making some of the mistakes I made and help you dig into the courage waiting to be discovered.

Whether your important message and unique wisdom remain locked in your heart forever or are shared with the world is your choice. If the dream is big enough, you'll do it. You'll write your book and put it out into the world. Deathbed regrets are not something I'd wish on anyone and I know you wouldn't wish them for yourself either. Bringing delight to the lives of others can leave you proud of the positive ripple that you've created through your writing.

You don't need to know *all* the answers before you begin. It's a step-by-step process and the stories shared in this book are an important step on that journey for you.

Before we dive in, there's a small disclaimer to share. In Australia, where I am, we use English from the United Kingdom, not the United States. So some words will have an extra L where a US reader feels it shouldn't. We use the letter U in words like "colour" and "honour". We sometimes use C where a US reader would use S, or S instead of Z. We end some words with T instead of ED. There are also some differences in the placement of commas, or the absence of them. It's not all about my imperfect 1984 high school English! These are just geographical variations. Don't let them distract you from the message and inspiration this book is here to offer.

1

MY PUBLISHING JOURNEY, SO FAR

My first book, *The Top Five Regrets of the Dying*, was birthed from that viral blog. A lovely agent in the USA, Jill, contacted me and asked if she could sign me up for a book on the subject. Since I was one of those people who always felt they'd write a book one day, I jumped at the chance. I knew nothing, and I mean *nothing*, about the publishing industry then. I explained that the only way I could tell the story was as a memoir, weaving my own journey through it. Otherwise, people wouldn't be open to hearing the message, as no one really wants to talk about death, let alone pay for a book on the subject. But if I talked about trying to create a life free of regret, then they'd connect with it.

Jill helped me to put a proposal together, which was a lesson in itself. You only need to google 'how to write a book proposal' these days and your answer's there. In fact, I just did and there are 297,000,000 results. There weren't many in early 2010, so Jill guided me on how to market the difference between my book and other titles already out there and explain why the publisher should choose me. It was a tight proposal, but the rejections poured in.

I was able to be released from that deal after our efforts were unsuccessful. Looking back, I feel I was being looked after from above. I would never sign a contract now without my lawyer looking over it. But I had no money at all at the time, having just surfaced from a period of severe burnout from all the years of looking after the dying, so I'd jumped at the opportunity. I'm grateful I could be released so soon. Not all agent agreements allow you that freedom unless it's negotiated at the start. I was signed to Jill for about a year. Often an agent will need you to sign for two years.

So I decided to self-publish. In the course of developing the proposal I'd created a book outline and since I was incapable of going back to caregiving, I decided to follow the signposts and venture down the author's track. I'll be talking more about self-publishing later in this book. It's an industry that has changed significantly and positively in the decade since I first went down that road. In 2011, there was a stigma attached to self-publishing, where most stores wouldn't even stock your book. If it hadn't been accepted by a publisher, it was labelled a dud before a page had been turned. This has thankfully changed.

I'm a late-in-life mum with one daughter. Her father and I separated when I was pregnant, so I've been a single mum from the start. I was blessed to conceive my daughter easily and birthed her when I was 45. It was the same time that my self-published book decided to take off – the *very* same time. Someone in a major global newspaper mentioned it and journalists from around the world were reaching out for interviews. As it had been such a hard road to get to the point where I received the kind of publicity that would get my message out there, including years as a singer/songwriter, I said yes to as many requests as possible. It was ridiculous. I was still doing interviews while in labour.

The night before my baby was born, with the labour pains becoming increasingly heavier, I finally closed the lid of my computer and put a very strong request out to the heavens: *Send help now or I'm quitting.*

It had taken me 14 years to become an overnight success, trying to make a living through creative endeavours while looking after the dying. I'd given all I had, but now I was going to be a mother and I wanted to be present for my babe. I was single and 45. This was my final opportunity to be a mum. I wasn't going to miss her life chasing a dream that now felt too much.

Obviously, someone, somewhere heard my prayer. Within 24 hours of my daughter being born, I was offered a publishing deal with my dream publishing house. I left the hospital with a gorgeous baby girl and a contract to sign – and that's when the advantages of a traditional publishing house kicked in. I sent them every enquiry I'd received about the translation rights to *The Top Five Regrets of the Dying*. They handled it all and my book went on to become the fastest foreign rights seller in their long and successful history.

As I mentioned, I've since sold the film rights to it as well. Additional requests around those rights came in afterwards, but I was happy with the film company I'd chosen. It's generally agents who'll try to sell your book to the film industry. I was grateful that the film companies came to me, instead of me having to go out looking.

These things do happen, and they could to you too. Very little about my publishing journey has been typical. Keep your heart open to positive surprises.

You still have to do the work, though! You need to show

life your commitment and turn up to write, do your research, face your fears, and do what you can to support your book to get out into the world. And then leave a little space for life to help.

2

A QUICK WORD ABOUT REJECTION

R ejection is not always personal. Publishing is a business and regardless of whether you have a healthy, enjoyable relationship with your publisher or not, they are not your best friend. They are a business partner. Money is always the driving force in the relationship for them and, let's face it, for you too. Even if your dream is just to be a published author, it helps if that dream will put food on your table.

When you consider how many thousands of submissions and enquiries publishing houses receive every month, it's worth giving thorough consideration to how you could improve your proposal before hitting the send button.

I'm not here to tell you how to write better, though I do offer some of my favourite tips later. I'm here to inform you of options, inspire you to try, and save you from making unnecessary mistakes or wasting your sacred time ... and your time *is* sacred: you're going to die and every day is one less of your life. It's time to get on with this dream of yours.

Due to the journey my own book has taken, from rejections and self-publishing to being traditionally published with a fabulous and respected global publishing house, I've come to view rejections with an open mind and heart.

It's certainly worth considering whether a stack of rejections is trying to tell you something about the quality of your writing. It wasn't until I started working closely with the editor on my second book, *Your Year for Change*, that I realised just how much the way I framed my message could be improved.

I learnt to say more with fewer words. Chapters benefitted when I moved paragraphs about, determining the best place for each. By finding the best choice of words, I improved a specific scene or even the whole book. Better descriptions gave a stronger sense of place. More attention to detail tightened the writing.

By keeping my heart open, letting go of resistance, and not taking feedback as a negative thing, I was able to improve my craft significantly. You can too.

But the quality of writing is only one of many reasons a traditional publishing house might reject you. Here are a few others:

- It's the wrong genre for the publisher.
- It features delicate subject matter not worth the potential hassle to them.
- You're an unknown author who hasn't expressed a vision for how you'll market your book.
- There's nothing unique about your perspective.
- The book contains colour images, which makes it too costly to print.
- The books doesn't fit the current or growing trend.

THE MAIN REASON for the first rejection I received was that they couldn't find a space in their current catalogue for something about death. I acknowledge, though, that the writing also needed improving. I was grateful to be able to do that for the updated edition of my book that my publisher released seven years later.

There are good things to learn from rejection. Consider where your proposal could be improved. Seek some guidance from a professional on the sample chapters you sent in. It doesn't need to cost a fortune. My first editor was a friend called Rob, who was a high school teacher. He looked over the manuscript and asked some questions that helped me see some areas that needed clarification.

Since I knew nothing about the publishing world, other than what I'd learnt through the rejection process so far, I decided to self-publish. I had some momentum, having already created the book outline, so there was no point in quitting. I certainly didn't have the energy to support dying people and their families anymore. I also loved the idea of working from home, something I am still grateful for all these years later.

A rejection is simply another step on your author's journey. It does not have to be the end – unless you allow it to be.

PUBLISHING – WHAT ARE YOUR OPTIONS?

When it comes to publishing, there are three main choices:

1. Traditional publishing.
2. Publishing via a self-publishing agency (also known as hybrid or vanity publishing).
3. Self-publishing.

Let's have a look at each of these.

TRADITIONAL PUBLISHING

Traditional publishers have great distribution channels, so the majority of books you see on the shelves in bookstores are through those. These are the publishers you submit your book proposal to for acceptance or rejection. Some will only accept submissions via an agent, and if you're an unknown author, an agent can be almost as challenging to secure as a direct deal with a publishing house.

Do your research. Look at books of the same genre to

yours and see who they're published by. Pay attention to the genres listed on each publisher's website. Their submission guidelines will be there too. Some open their doors to submissions once a month. Browse the spines of books on bookstore shelves and pay attention to which publisher put them out into the world.

The main benefit of a traditional publisher is that your book will usually be seen by more people, especially in the first few months of release. You don't need to learn all the ropes of distribution yourself. You become a part of a team.

A traditional publishing house can also represent you to foreign agencies. Of course, this means they get a healthy cut of any of the royalties from translations. (As would an agent marketing it for you to international brokers. There are foreign rights agencies that specialise in these things. Book fairs and other author conferences can be good places to connect with them.)

There are also disadvantages to your book going out into the world through a traditional publisher, which is why some successful, traditionally published authors are now moving to self-publishing.

One is that you don't really have a final say in the cover design. That may not sound like such a big problem, but it takes courage to let go and trust someone else to represent your creation, especially if it's your first book. You may get to influence the cover design to a degree, but it's still the publisher's final choice.

I was given two images to consider for my third book, *Bloom*. I chose one and my publisher put the other on the cover. There was nothing I could do beyond letting them know of my disappointment. Some authors may have more say with their book covers, but established publishing houses have their own design departments. They specialise in watching the market, following trends and creating new ones. So, as an author, there needs to be a little bit of letting go of your precious work. In the end, the cover for *Bloom* turned out to be lovely. Once the text had been added, in well-designed fonts, it changed everything. I don't think my first choice would have actually worked so well.

Through a traditional publisher, you also have to work with the editor assigned to you. I've had a beautiful experience with one editor, where I felt incredibly understood, respected and supported. I've also felt a complete disconnect with another editor, yet we had to see the project through together. We were both speaking English but coming at the book from such varying angles that it was like we each spoke a different language. Still, we learn what we're meant to in life and the experience strengthened me in other ways.

The main disadvantage to publishing traditionally is the much lower percentage you get of the book's sale price as royalties. For a paperback, for example, it could be the difference between receiving $1.50 for each book sold via traditional publishing compared to $10 per book when you sell it yourself directly from your website – depending on your price and printing costs, of course.

It's not always this straightforward, though. A thousand books sold in stores to people who weren't looking for your book specifically could still make you $1150. Those thousand people might never have known your name without the physical shop to stroll into during their lunchbreak. Receiving $10 per book doesn't add up to anything if they're not selling. (We'll touch on marketing later.)

A thing I love about being traditionally published with my non-fiction books is the great reduction in the amount of administration. While I still have to go through each step of a book's journey from creation to release in a systemised way with my publisher, I'm not dealing with returns, refunds, damages or delays through delivery, or micro-managing the whole process.

I receive a statement every six months which details the sales of each book in each country. I send them an invoice for the total listed and the money arrives in my account. There's no other administration necessary once I've jumped through the hoops to get my book out there in the first place. And throughout the process, I'm supported by an amazing group of people who are also invested in my project.

PUBLISHING VIA A SELF-PUBLISHING agency

These are also known as vanity agencies, vanity press or hybrid publishing. There are some disadvantages to this option, but again, advantages too.

Most self-publishing agencies will accept anyone's work. Some will rave about how special your book is just to get you to sign with them. Don't be fooled. Most will publish anything. Their profit comes through the setting up of your book in the system, and your willingness to pay heavily for that.

In many cases, you'll receive a few copies of your book in the agreed deal and then have to purchase any more that you need. The companies' profits and survival are usually not dependent on how many books you sell. It's the hefty upfront fees that keep them going.

It's not all bad, though. Some people don't have the energy or knowledge to self-publish, or the energy to get the knowledge, and this option at least gets their book released. You often get a cover design included, and some of these publishers offer editing services. While there are some questionable operators out there, some very professional and worthwhile services also exist.

It's a middle option between being traditionally published or taking the reins fully in self-publishing.

When I say that I self-published my first book, this is how I initially did it: by spending a lump sum upfront just to get my book out there. I had no idea where to start, so it helped. When you have a book wanting to be birthed, you look for whatever options you can and there weren't many then. Thanks to social media algorithms and my searching for all the right keywords, a self-publishing agency advertisement popped up in front of me, with all the enticing copy.

I don't regret it. It got my book out there, even though I'd never choose this option again. For busy people whose focus is on other things, it can be a good option.

Self-publishing agencies generally have two printing choices. These also apply to self-publishing without an agency. One is called print on demand (or POD) and the other is to pay for printing costs upfront. POD is amazing these days. When a customer orders your book online, the system prints a copy automatically and, within a few days, it is in the post to them. The resources listed at the back of this book will help you navigate the system choices.

A few of my friends are speakers who are happy to lug their books along to every event. They've chosen to pay for printing upfront through a self-publishing agency and are happy with their decision. Their agency was professional, had great editors and designers, and supported them all the way through. These friends are speakers who have also become authors. Most of their sales come through their audience at speaking gigs, not through bookstores. I'm the opposite: an author who also speaks at events.

With all the advances in technology since I self-published in 2011, there is always advice to help make your final decision as informed as possible. Sometimes it can be overwhelming for a budding author, though. That's why I'm bringing this little book into creation.

Thoroughly read the fine print of any contract with a vanity publisher. Some can be quite restrictive – and you don't need to be trying to recoup your investment for years to come. The same applies if you strike a deal with a traditional publishing house. Just because you don't understand a legal sentence doesn't mean it's irrelevant. The legal jargon in contracts can be difficult to understand – that's why there are lawyers that specialise in untangling them.

Also, research reviews of the self-publishing agency before signing anything. When you do a search of the publisher's name with the word 'reviews' after it, you might find yourself breathing a sigh of relief that you haven't yet signed to them. Or you might have your fears eased by the positive reviews left by others – assuming they're genuine reviews and not from people working for the publishing house. When you do such a search, you may also come across comparison websites, which will help you make a clearer choice.

Self-publishing

To self-publish means to steer the whole ship your own way. While you'll be paying out a small percentage of your profits for some of your technical systems, the bulk of your book sales is yours to keep. You also receive the funds quickly, not having to wait six months for royalties from your publisher.

There are many systems and choices available. It's worth researching all you can to find what fits for you. Remember, too, that technology improves all the time, and a decision on a program to distribute your books now does not have to be permanent. It's an ever-evolving industry. Things will change.

If you wish to release your book as a paperback, it needs to be at least 24 pages for you to use the print on demand system.

Many bookstores are willing to stock independent releases these days, particularly if their audience is already asking for your title or if you're local and develop an association with them. Your book can also be marketed from your website and through major online retailers.

Don't forget ebooks, which are worthy income streams, even if the profit appears to be less than from a paperback. Once an ebook is formatted and uploaded, that seed is planted to bloom forever.

And of course, in this busy world, many readers *hear* books more than read them, due to the culture of audiobooks.

I've chosen to self-publish the fiction series I'm currently working on because I love the idea of owning it completely. I'm still using the services of an editor and a cover designer, both of whom I consider significant contributors to any book's potential success, but the ongoing decisions remain my own. As they are short stories, there are not enough pages in each book to print. So they'll be released as ebooks and audiobooks. Depending on the final page count of the whole series, I'll likely combine them into one printed version at the end.

What I'm planning to do is to sell the ebooks from my website first and a little later open sales avenues to include selling directly (but not exclusively) through Amazon and then through a distributor for other online stores, such as Apple Books. This is to cut out the middleman as much as possible, while also not creating such a volume of administration and maintenance that there's no time left to actually write new books.

The audiobooks will likely only be available through my website, at least initially. It's a decision still forming, but I'm less inclined to lean only on a major distributor in a world and industry that continue to change. Selling directly will also help my audience learn that the earliest releases of my independent books will always be from my website.

The company I am using to deliver the ebooks and (possibly) audiobooks through my website also looks after all enquiries from customers. This is very attractive to my time management.

After much research, my decision around the paperbacks (print on demand books) is for customers to order through their local independent bookstore or Amazon. While I could sell them directly from my website, I don't want to be dealing with questions from customers about the printing or delivery. Not because I don't love my customers. I do! But I want to spend time writing, not attending to additional administration or training a team member to manage it. This decision may change later when I see how much money I am losing from not selling them directly from my site or when my load has lessened in other areas and I can give more time to it. Or I may look at the figures and consider it a great decision and well worth the money going out to the middle-man because of the time I've saved.

There are a vast number of options for self-publishing

these days. If you do want to follow in the footsteps of my friends and pay upfront for your printing costs, you can. If you would prefer to use print on demand, there are businesses that specialise in this, with distribution links and delivery services in place. A customer can buy from your website, but you never have to physically handle the book.

There are agencies that look after narrating and audiobook distribution, or you may want to narrate your own. I narrated my non-fiction books and am glad I did. Many listeners love it when the author narrates their own book. I'd already had a lot of interview experience by then, though, so the microphone and I were friends. Only you can decide whether your voice is the best one for your book. I'm not sure that I'll narrate my first novel when it gets to that stage. I think a specialist could bring it to life with more feeling.

With so many choices out there, especially once you start listening to self-publishing podcasts and googling every question that comes up, it can become overwhelming rather than encouraging.

Start simple. You don't need every answer yet. Some authors start off by simply selling their books as PDFs via a digital store. A small start is always better than none.

There's a major shift underway back to self-publishing. It's no longer judged to be a last-ditch option. Many successful authors see it as the first. The advances in technology and the desire for full ownership and autonomy support this. Like every kind of publishing, it has its pros and cons.

Higher profit margins may come with more administration, particularly in the beginning. More office work could detract from the actual creation of books. Set goals and try to be disciplined around this. Never forget that you're doing all this because of a love of expressing yourself through writing.

Another advantage of self-publishing is that you can write about topics you connect with, even if they might be too sensitive for a publisher to take the risk on. You may find your interests are quite niche. Write to that niche. Don't try to please everyone. A small, loyal audience who totally loves your subject matter is far stronger in the long term than a book written for an audience who'll read anything that comes at a 99c bargain but will forget you just as quickly.

The Top Five Regrets of the Dying filled a niche that I didn't realise needed filling. Back then, I don't think the word 'niche' was even in my consciousness. I knew what it meant but it had never held any relevance in my world. And then, wham! I've written something that struck global hearts without even knowing I was going to. Sometimes ignorance truly is bliss. If I'd known how many people were going to read that first book, I might have been scared off.

When you self-publish, all the decisions are yours – which you may find both enticing and terrifying.

There's much to learn from whichever publishing path you choose, or whichever chooses you. But don't forget the good stuff – it's an amazing feeling to hold your finished work in your hand.

4

ACKNOWLEDGING THE MILESTONES

The more you can see your writing and publishing journey as an adventure, the more present you'll be to notice the milestones you achieve. Where other people are up to on their writing path doesn't need to be at all relevant to you. We're all here to learn different lessons in life and all successful writers were once beginners. Just focus on your own steps. Otherwise you risk denying yourself enjoyment and the satisfaction of achieving each positive step.

When the self-published version of *The Top Five Regrets of the* Dying was released, I didn't stop to acknowledge my achievement. Even though it had been rejected by 25 publishers, I'd actually achieved something just by being signed to a literary agent. Considering I was a singer/songwriter and a blogger at the time, this was a great accomplishment in itself. I'd also been trying to find my way into creative self-employment for well over a decade by then, so any progress was worthy of notice.

To have a traditional publishing deal offered to me was incredible, but I was too distracted at the time by single-parenting a newborn baby. It was a few years before I came up for air and truly noticed what I'd done.

Prior to that, the viral blog had heralded a whirlwind of change. I enjoyed that time, especially the surprise that perhaps my writing career wasn't to be through songs, but the written word. I often shook my head in wonder – I never saw it coming. It turns out that being an author suits me so much better than slogging it out with my inspirational folk songs in loud pubs, with drinkers only interested in the sports TV up on the wall.

The publishing deal had arrived with my baby, and so did rheumatoid arthritis. So when my publisher asked for a second book a year or so later, the best I could do was a collection of short stories. I was single-parenting in crippling chronic pain. It was a time of survival rather than creative inspiration.

I sent that book, *Your Year for Change*, out into the world with hardly any attention or love. Even when some of my readers wrote in to say it was their favourite of mine, I couldn't absorb anything about the achievement of writing it.

It wasn't until I was narrating the audiobook for it several years later that I realised what a beautiful book it was. I could finally be proud of it – and I am. In fact, of the three non-fiction books I've traditionally published, I think it is now my own personal favourite. *Bloom* is my third book and is about surrender and courage. Like *The Top Five Regrets of the Dying*, it also sells better than *Your Year for Change*, but that middle child is now much-loved.

The author's path is not always about the dollars. Or perhaps I should say, it's not *only* about the dollars. I'm a single mum. Writing is my main form of income. Of course, it's about the dollars! But not only. It's about the courage to express yourself honestly. It's what you learn about yourself as you break through each new layer of fear and reach deeper into yourself. It's a loving service to your audience. It's who you become in the process. And a part of that is pausing to acknowledge the milestones, regardless of how small you may judge them to be.

I learnt that the hard way, but have mastered it now. When a new opportunity comes my way, whether I decide to accept it or not, I remember my beginnings. I reflect on how much courage I've found over the decades, and how many challenges I've overcome to honour my creative dreams, and I say, "Well done!".

I also say "thank you" every time I receive payment for my work. It doesn't matter how big your first payment is. Just acknowledge that someone believes in your creation enough to part with their money, that they'll be sharing time with you through the pages you wrote, and that any enjoyment or benefit that ripples through their life as a result of your book is due to your courage and willingness to take action.

Every forward step is positive. What may appear to be a backward step – and there will be some of those too – doesn't have to be considered negative. It can just be another step in a dance to get you where you want to go. Remember, we learn through our mistakes, so don't judge them too harshly. See them as loving signposts that help you get clearer on your direction.

Success isn't just holding your book in your hands for the first time, though of course that's a very cool feeling, as I mentioned. Success is also just finding the courage to have a go.

People will judge you, but that says more about them than you. Since you're on ever-reducing time, does their opinion truly need to hold any power? (They're going to die too, if that's any consolation.) Listen to your own heart. If you have a book in you that wants to come out and be shared, then please get on with it. Regret is a painful experience to die with – and an even more painful one to live with. The reins are in your hands. Use them to steer in the right direction.

If I'd listened to everyone who mocked me in my life and career, I might still be wearing uncomfortable high heels working behind a counter at a bank, wondering how all those other people could be outside on a glorious sunny day when I couldn't. Now I'm one of those people. I have a choice around when to write and when to take a walk. I still exercise discipline around my writing, definitely, but there's flexibility in my time too.

Early in my career, I contacted an author's organisation in Australia with a question or two. Somewhere during the conversation, the man told me how few writers make a living from it in this country. I told him I was going to buy a house with the proceeds of my writing. He said he hoped I was willing to live in a tent.

You may hear all sorts of opinions like this. Don't subscribe to them and don't allow others to set the rules for your life. I bought a house from my writing. Then I bought 30 remote, hilltop acres with views that go on forever, which I'm putting a tiny home on. The only *tent* is for my daughter and her friends to camp outside for fun. This is the result of courage.

5

MARKETING IS NOT A DIRTY WORD

In the old days, securing a traditional publishing deal also meant an organised book tour on your behalf, as well as lots of other publicity. Those days are gone. A traditional publisher will certainly support the launch of your book by securing as much publicity for it as possible, through interviews and other opportunities. However, it's up to you as the author to support your book's growth alongside that launch period and then beyond.

Social media and mailing lists

Not only does the majority of the marketing fall to the author, the traditional publishers often need to see that you have an existing platform, through a mailing list and social media pages. In most cases, they need to see that publishing your book is a sure thing and doesn't run the risk of loss.

Of course, rules can be broken. One author friend of mine scored a three-book deal with a major publishing house in Australia by showing up at a book conference and pitching her first book directly to a publisher. She still has a very limited presence on social media and has not started collecting email addresses for a mailing list. This is another example of how rules can be broken.

Generally, though, if you're trying for a traditional publishing deal because you want to see your book on the shelves at the airport bookstore, then you need to grow your audience through interaction, campaigns, free giveaways, and developing trust with them. Sharing little snippets and short stories early on in your career can help with this.

Some authors are prolific in showing up on social media and do most of their business there, building relationships through interaction. Many others don't, especially given that plenty of authors are deeply introverted. I love observing extroverted authors and seeing how naturally they interact, given how hard I had to work to become comfortable with social media myself.

Growing your audience and getting them aware of your books is a daunting process for the majority of writers. Some folks are natural marketers. I'm not. Instead, I've learnt how to work with what fits me most comfortably. This has come through much trial and error.

I have social media pages on Facebook, Instagram and YouTube. It's better to do two or three platforms well than try for all of them, creating heavy obligations. Choose the ones you enjoy the most.

The social media platforms own your audience on their sites. If they crash and disappear, like MySpace did, or change their algorithms and make it almost impossible to reach your audience unless you pay for ads, then all the hard work of building those relationships could be gone.

I haven't used social media ads for years but may do for my fiction series. The algorithms are no longer as favourable for reaching your potential audience unless you're paying.

Social media ads can bring a lot of business if the campaign is designed by someone who understands that world.

It's my mailing list that is always my priority, though. I own that list. While I value my social media audiences and now enjoy the interaction with them, it is my fortnightly newsletter that I show up for consistently. I have a sign-up form to the list at the bottom of every page of my website, as well as links from all of my social media pages.

Mailing lists are golden. They're your most dedicated followers. They've parted with their email address for your correspondence. They've come to trust you – and trust is needed for people to buy.

INTERVIEWS – **why they're useful, and when to say yes**

Mailing lists and social media are not the only avenues for marketing. Interviews can be fabulous for exposing your work to a new audience.

When my blog first took off, I was receiving numerous interview requests daily. Since I'd already been trying to find self-employment through being a singer/songwriter, I had a little practice with interviews. I'm grateful for that. No skills we ever learn in life are wasted. They're all supporting us for our bigger dreams, in one way or another. My banking career in my early adult years, for example, gave me skills that have been invaluable in the administrative side of my writing career. Some of your existing skills will support your steps as an author.

The interview requests continued once the book was released, and have ever since. Sometimes I receive invitations for an interview more to do with my other books, my health journey, or parenting. These can be a lovely change because most of the hosts interviewing me about *The Top*

Five Regrets of the Dying ask the same or very similar questions. After over a decade of that, it's always a relief to realise I'm speaking with a host who's actually done some research and asks fascinating questions. It's much better for the listening audience too, as the conversation becomes unique.

A good interview can expose your work to more people than hundreds of dollars' worth of social media ads. The listener also has time to get to know you before deciding to buy your book. It's not just an ad that keeps popping up as they mindlessly scroll through their feed.

When I first started out, I said yes to almost every interview request. Now I say no to most. I needed a break from the same conversations but also, they take up a lot of time. I'm a single mum with a small window of writing time. I have to write within that and around my energy. If I give all of that time away, I'll never get to do what really lights me up. It's a dance, really. Sometimes it's writing mode. Sometimes it needs to be about promotion and administration.

One thing to consider if you're asked to be interviewed is how many listeners are going to hear the conversation. Many new podcast hosts are looking for guests to get their show rolling, but there may be very few listeners. That's OK if you're not seasoned with interviews yet. Enjoy the conversations and use them to master your story and interview technique.

Leave space for the host to ask questions by keeping your replies as concise as possible. That may mean a story you tell takes three minutes instead of fifteen. Let the host steer the ship and let yourself be surprised by where the conversation goes. One good question can open up a whole new direction.

Sometimes it only takes one listener, the right listener, for you to gain useful support for your writing. A local bookstore owner may hear the interview, for example, and invite you to speak about your book in their store. Every forward step is important, no matter its size.

If you're looking for interviews, join some online business groups and ask if anyone is looking for guests for their shows. Business Chicks is a well-known women's business group in Australia. (You don't have to run your own business to join). I sometimes see people looking for guests in other women's business groups I'm in on social media too.

There are many groups on both social media and direct websites where people with similar interests support each other. Do a search for your region or state and see what can be found.

Sometimes, these connections move into real life and other times they remain as online relationships for years. Business groups are a fabulous way to not only get your work out there but also to make contacts in other areas that may overlap with your work.

One of the first business groups I ever joined was about a hundred local women who had all done the same online business course. Through that, I not only made great friends but also found a graphic designer, an accountant, a social media advertisement specialist and most of what else I needed at the time.

Let the new connections know what your specialty is. It might be western romance, or how to sleep better. You might have had unique experiences travelling to a remote jungle and photographing the creatures there, or it might be a more familiar story, but something in your own history makes it unique. Perhaps just getting to the point of writing the book was a huge achievement, so find podcasts that might value that subject matter.

Many of the biggest podcast hosts are bombarded with guest submissions, so don't take it personally if you don't hear back from them. Some need to see that you have an existing audience, so you can both cross-promote the interview.

The biggest mistake I made in the early days of interviews for my books was giving my time to people who didn't respect it. A woman with a decent audience didn't show up at the time we had agreed and sent no apology. When she contacted me a week later and set a new time, I turned up and did the interview. These days there would be no second chance. My time is as important as theirs and if they don't respect mine, they don't get it.

A news reader from a large TV broadcasting channel in America once set a time with me for an interview. It was 4 am my time and I was only a couple of weeks from birthing my daughter. Despite needing as much rest as possible, I had myself ready before 4 am, all professional and presentable. He didn't show up. When he got in touch about 5 hours later, he said there had been a more important news story and requested that I record half an hour of content and send it to him. I don't know if you remember how slow sending videos was a decade ago. It took about four hours to transfer the video *after* making it. There was no thanks or further contact from him, and they only used 10 seconds of it. Yes, 10 seconds. When he got in touch for another interview a couple of years later, I declined.

I've had countless people say to my assistant, "But I only want half an hour of her time". It's never just half an hour when you factor in the scheduling, putting other things on hold, and getting ready physically and mentally. These days I do a very small handful of free interviews and only with large media outlets or established podcast hosts, and I offer a few paid spots for those who are determined to have me on their show.

Getting to that point has taken years of work. So I don't recommend writing interview opportunities off as quickly as that if you're new to the game. Find gratitude for the invitation and master that craft in the process. When you connect with a host, it can also be a fabulous personal experience. I've left interviews in tears of joy from the beautiful conversation that unfolded.

Marketing can scare authors, but if your book has the potential to bring enjoyment to the reader's life, you can promote it from the perspective of service. It may feel more natural that way.

6

WRITING TIPS

As I bravely announced at the start of this book, I'm not the best author on the planet. I'm not the worst either. As with any skill, you get better with practice. Writing is a lifelong evolution. You can always improve. So, I'm going to share some of my favourite lessons so far to support your writing.

SHOW, **don't tell**

This means to allow the reader to fill in the gaps.

To tell is to write: "It was a freezing day. The temperature had already dropped below zero. She walked down the grey street."

To show is to write: "She wrapped her scarf tighter but it made little difference. Through the windows, people at restaurant tables talked and laughed. She bent her head to the wind and walked on."

Paint the scene with your words rather than writing a factual news report. Allow the reader to *feel* the setting.

. . .

DRAFT WITH YOUR HEART, **revise with your head**

A personal favourite tip, which still shapes most of what I write, comes from the movie *Finding Forrester*. Sean Connery's character says, "You write your first draft with your heart and you rewrite with your head. The first key to writing is to write, not to think." I summarise it, when reminding myself, down to, "Write the first draft with your heart, the second with your head." If you can get your head out of the way and allow that first draft to spill unhindered, then you already have the raw material on which to build.

CONNECT **with your reader's emotions**

More than anything, your writing needs to touch the emotions of the reader. Does this book about writing and publishing only give you facts or does it make you a little excited, scared, hopeful, or all of that? If the excitement scares you a little, that's OK. It means you're taking this dream seriously. No one who has ever enjoyed success has done so without facing their fear along the way. Myself included.

Whether you're writing non-fiction or fiction, you're telling a story that needs to connect with the reader's emotions somehow. Even the most factual books need to touch the reader's feelings in order to stay interesting. Pick the freshest angle you can.

KEEP **your writing concise**

Is every word necessary? If you learn to show rather than tell, you'll find the need for explanation reduced. Equally, the need for adjectives and adverbs lessens. A good sentence will tell enough on its own. That's not to say I never use descriptive words. I do, because sometimes I simply love to! Some words used to describe a moment can be delightful, like "convivial" or "serendipitous".

OWN your voice

Trust in its individual expression, while always trying to improve it.

KEEP it simple

Using big words that are unnecessary but make you feel clever is rarely helpful or enjoyable for the reader. Use them only if they're the absolute best word for the situation.

Consider the word "solicitude", for example. A sentence could read, "Her solicitude was well-intended but rather intense." That works OK, but so does, "Her concern was a little overbearing, though well-intended."

They both work, and that's where the beauty of your individual voice comes in. Ask yourself often as you're writing: which is truly the best word? You get to choose which to use in creating an image or feeling for the reader.

It's a fabulous craft and an honour. It is also a cathartic healing process. As you find your voice, you step more into your own power. You become more grounded in who you are and how you want to express yourself in the world.

USE the senses in your writing

If you want to create imagery, don't just stick with the sense of sight. Perhaps the waft of a rose's scent catches the character's attention. Right there, the reader understands the moment. They feel it more than see it. They can smell that rose.

An extroverted friend of mine can only write his books in cafes. He says he can't write without the aroma of coffee and the noise of people. It helps to keep his senses alive. He needs to be reminded of every sense, or he falls into the trap of only writing about sight and sound.

As an introvert, I'm perfectly happy to stay home and write. My computer is on a cushion on my lap, my legs are elevated and covered with a woollen rug. The fire burns nearby, a chihuahua sleeps between my calves, and a curly cavoodle is on a cushion nearby. Beside me sits my pottery mug of chai. The spices and tea have been slowly brewed with fresh ginger and then enhanced by a little honey at the end. The fire burns slowly while the dogs dream. Only the occasional tick from the fire or a distant passing car can be heard.

Now you're in the room with me. It doesn't need to look exactly the same in your mind as the way I see it, because we both *feel* it. Never underestimate the importance of using the senses in your writing.

STAY FLEXIBLE, **but in control**

You're driving this project. Try to steer it in the right direction.

Most creative projects will take on a life of their own. That can be surprising in the best ways, but not if the project goes off on such a merry adventure that the core message gets left behind.

CONSIDER HIRING **an editor**

Editors are usually a very good investment. As the author, you can become too close to your own work. An editor can look at it through fresh eyes, with the wisdom of experience in language and grammar. It's not a weakness to have someone help tighten up your style. It's giving your book the best support possible before it flies out into the world. Do your research and choose an editor who you feel drawn to, someone with existing credentials in your genre. They'll see things you won't.

Your book is like a child. Give it the best possible start in life that you can.

7

DO YOU WANT TO DIE WITH REGRETS?

I f you wait for perfection, you're denying yourself the experience of completing your book and sending it out into the world. It's a very fine feeling to see your dream through to completion – and a huge improvement on the heart-wrenching pain of regret.

Make your book as good as possible, for where you are now in your writing, and send it on its way. Every mum or dad improves their parenting skills with each child, but that doesn't make them ashamed of their first. Let it be the same for you. Each book may improve on the previous one, but each is still something to be proud of. Be grateful instead of embarrassed or ashamed, since you're improving in your craft all the time. And who knows? That first book may even change many lives. It will certainly change yours.

There comes a time when you need to let it go out into the world. When you step out into the public eye with your work, you're putting yourself in a vulnerable position. You open yourself to judgment, especially by people who haven't had the guts to honour their own dreams. There will always be cynics. You either give them your power or step into your own.

Remember, you're going to die. Your time is sacred, and so are your dreams. They are the vision of your heart and a quiet whisper of what you're capable of.

I wish you the courage to honour that call.

RESOURCES

As mentioned earlier in this book, technology is improving all the time and what suits your needs now may not later. I've been hesitant to share specific systems here for that reason – they can become outdated quickly. But I also know that just having something to research, or a small stepping stone to get you started, can make a massive difference when you have absolutely no idea where to start.

So these are some of the systems worth considering if you're going to sell your own books. While Amazon is the natural consideration for most, it is not the only one. Amazon offers options for you to be exclusive to them with your ebooks, or you can choose for them to be just one of the stores you sell through. If you're exclusive to them, they promote your books more, but you can also pay for ads if you're non-exclusive. Many of the technical systems below also have the option to pay for ads within their systems, to gain better publicity.

If you choose to be non-exclusive – which is the option that sits better for me personally – then you're what's called 'wide'. You have gone wide with your book/s. You may sell directly from your own website or storefront, where you cut out the middleman, or you can use a distributor to represent your books to other online stores, saving you potential administration headaches. You can also do both: sell directly from your website and to Amazon and then use a distribution service for other stores. Naturally, having a middleman is a paid service so a percentage of your sale price would be shared with those distributors. It all depends on how much time you want to spend on the administrative side of things.

Here are some systems as a starting point -

For print-on demand (POD) paperbacks:
Bookvault
Lulu
IngramSpark – best if you also want your book in real-life bookshops

Online shopfronts:
Shopify – a monthly fee to operate, has print integrations with some companies, like Bookvault.
Payhip – a percentage taken from every sale, with no monthly fee. Integrations through BookFunnel for ebooks and audiobooks. No printing options.
WooCommerce through a WordPress website – many variables possible

Delivery to your online store for distribution:
BookFunnel (including audiobooks)

Distribution to online stores if you're not selling directly to them yourself:

Draft2Digital
IngramSpark
Findaway Voices (audiobooks)

Email providers for your mailing list:
Mailchimp – no longer integrates well with Shopify
Omnisend
Klaviyo
(And many, *many* others!)

Graphics for marketing:
Canva
MockupShots

Podcasts:
Mark Dawson's Self Publishing Formula
The Creative Penn (Joanna Penn also has lots of great resources for the independent author, including for marketing)

There may be a lot of industry jargon in these podcasts that makes no sense to you initially. Just take in what you can. The more you listen, the more you'll understand.

I recommend starting with The Creative Penn's interview with Erin Wright, who shares valuable information and runs a Facebook group called Wide for the Win. The group is very active, with experienced authors supporting new writers by answering their questions. But even the interview alone will offer great insights into what's possible with self-publishing. There is also an interview with Morgana Best who has been publishing directly from her own website for years.

And, of course, my website offers inspiration to keep you focused: bronnieware.com

ABOUT THE AUTHOR

Bronnie Ware is the author of the international bestselling memoir *The Top Five Regrets of the Dying*, published in 32 languages, with a movie in the pipeline.

She is a TEDx speaker and has been interviewed by Wall St Journal, ABC Radio National, The Guardian, The Sunday Times, Harvard Business Review, and hundreds of publications worldwide.

She has also been interviewed on numerous podcasts including by Dr Wayne Dyer, Marie Forleo, Fearne Cotton, Lewis Howes, Dr Rangan Chatterjee, and Tami Simon.

Bronnie lives in rural Australia and is a respected teacher of courage on the global stage. She is an advocate for simplicity and leaving space to breathe, drawing on courage to follow the heart and allow life to provide the shortcuts.

To find out more about Bronnie's teachings, visit bronnieware.com

ALSO BY BRONNIE WARE

The Top Five Regrets of the Dying: A Life Transformed by the Dearly Departing

Your Year for Change: 52 Reflections for Regret-Free Living

Bloom: A Tale of Courage, Surrender, and Breaking Through Upper Limits

From 25 Rejections to a Million Readers: Essential Tips for Budding Authors

The Purple Chair: An inspirational, short-story, fiction series celebrating the fragility and strength of being human (Coming in late 2023/early 2024)

The Top Five Regrets of the Dying - Digital Card Deck

Inspirational Prints to enhance your home

Read more from Bronnie at bronnieware.com